A Christian's Life Purpose

A Guide to Finding Your Purpose in Life

by Kathleen Bishopson

Table of Contents

Introduction 1

Chapter 1: Our Five Physical Purposes 7

Chapter 2: Your Five Spiritual Purposes 13

Chapter 3: When Finding Your Purpose Becomes Difficult 21

Chapter 4: Showing Off Your Purpose 25

Conclusion 29

Introducing my book 'Disciplining a Defiant Child' 33

Introduction

Life's purpose is a very vast subject to discuss. There are loads of available books around to help you discover the reasons why you are here on Earth. However, finding, reading, and comparing the information in all these books would take forever and before you actually discover your purpose, you may be out of time.

The Bible is the best source of answers to this simple, yet very complicated question. For life simply comes from God and He alone is the very own author of each breath. That's why His words and His principles should become the mere foundation of our existence, the road that everyone should follow and the gift that we should always be ready to enjoy. For God has given us life to enjoy and celebrate it with Him.

Yet, everyday of our live and sometimes our whole beings are challenged: physically, mentally, emotionally and spiritually. Each and everyone face different tests, and experiences every second of the day to measure and figure out our strength and weaknesses. The main goal in facing these circumstances seems to be simply to survive, so that after that we can face another challenge that awaits us again.

But the question remains the same: *WHY?* Why do you have to fight in order to survive? And What's the whole point or purpose?

There are two ways to define your purpose in life, which are by your physical purpose and your spiritual purpose respectively. These two things co-exist together, written by God to appear parallel in nature. Through these things, we were created and born. Genesis 2:7 said that God formed the man through dust, and then he breathed him with life. And that's how we are destined to live a life while we consider both of our physical and spiritual purpose.

© Copyright 2014 by LCPublifish LLC - All rights reserved.

This document is geared towards providing exact and reliable information in regard to the topic and issue covered. The publication is sold with the idea that the publisher is not required to render accounting, officially permitted, or otherwise, qualified services. If advice is necessary, legal or professional, a practiced individual in the profession should be ordered.

- From a Declaration of Principles which was accepted and approved equally by a Committee of the American Bar Association and a Committee of Publishers and Associations.

In no way is it legal to reproduce, duplicate, or transmit any part of this document in either electronic means or in printed format. Recording of this publication is strictly prohibited and any storage of this document is not allowed unless with written permission from the publisher. All rights reserved.

The information provided herein is stated to be truthful and consistent, in that any liability, in terms of inattention or otherwise, by any usage or abuse of any policies, processes, or directions contained within is the solitary and utter responsibility of the recipient reader. Under no circumstances will any legal responsibility or blame be held against the publisher for any reparation, damages, or monetary loss due to the information herein, either directly or indirectly.

Respective authors own all copyrights not held by the publisher.

The information herein is offered for informational purposes solely, and is universal as so. The presentation of the information is without contract or any type of guarantee assurance.

The trademarks that are used are without any consent, and the publication of the trademark is without permission or backing by the trademark owner. All trademarks and brands within this book are for clarifying purposes only and are the owned by the owners themselves, not affiliated with this document.

Chapter 1: Our Five Physical Purposes

Remember that man was created through dust and later on he became flesh when empowered by the spirit of God. So, since we are human and we are made with flesh, we are intended to live in the world just like a human should: to eat, to sleep and to wake up and go about our daily habits. But God placed us here not just to simply go through our daily routine of living, but rather to make a difference and to fulfill a deeper role too.

To get married and multiply

In Genesis 1:28, Adam and Eve were instructed by God to live together and multiply. Our bodies are specially designed by God to reproduce human life that will become the next generation. So, *sex* is a wonderful gift from the Lord. However, some people are actually degrading the actual meaning of this precious gift as they disrespect its true purpose. It is natural for humans to appreciate sex, however, doing this out of marriage is a sin. It should be a special act reserved for a married couple who shares love with one another and may bear offspring whom they will raise for His glory.

So, one of your physical purpose here is to find your mate so you can experience this wonderful pleasure together in the *right time*. You are shaped to build and take good care of your own family. This means that once you've decided to marry someone, be sure you are physically, emotionally and financially ready and secure.

However, not everyone was called to get married. Instead, you may choose to stay single for the rest of your life. It is your choice and nothing is wrong with that. But the Bible tells us clearly in 1 Corinthians 6:18, to flee from any sexual immorality. That's why if you choose to remain and to devote yourself into singledom, try not to fall into temptation to remain clean and pure in the sight of God especially when it comes to this very sensitive matter. 1 Corinthians 7:8-9 says it is good to stay unmarried but if a man cannot control himself, he should marry then, since it is better to get married than to fall into temptation of the burning flesh.

To honor your father and your mother

Your parents are the instruments used by God to give you life. Because of them, you were born and are now experiencing the wonders of this life! Whether you've been blessed with loving parents or irresponsible parents, you are instructed by God to respect and honor them. For doing this, you are destined to receive two great promises as Ephesians 6:2-3 says, *"Honor your father and mother, so that it may go well with you and that you may enjoy long life on the earth."* He wants us to achieve these "physical rewards" while we are still here on earth. That's why we are supposed to make our parents happy and proud!

To become rich and successful

"For I know the plans I have for you," declares the Lord, "plans to prosper you and not to harm you, plans to give you hope and a future." –JEMERIAH 29:11

Since God is our Father, He wants us to become rich and successful in every aspect of our lives. So, providing us with fortune to have a good shelter, enough food, and proper clothing is one of His major priorities for us. It is not really a sin if you were born poor and homeless, but if you are still poor and homeless when you die, then that's a sin! Because you were provided with knowledge, strength and good health by God and yet you did not used them to fulfill your purpose. Just like any other parents in the world, God wants his children to become rich and successful here on earth.

To become a good steward

Are you an employee or a business owner? A rich man or even a poor one? Do you have millions in assets or do you only have a single cent in your pocket? No matter how big or small your possessions are, they come from the Lord and He wants us to be a good steward of His blessings. In Genesis 1:28, God has given man the supreme authority over all His creations on earth and He is expecting us to take care of all these things. Hence, it is our duty and purpose to preserve and take care of nature just as much as we take care of ourselves.

Moreover, it is not a coincidence that you are in a particular situation right now. No matter how badly you feel about your work, for example, be thankful about it. Because your purpose is to take good care of your job and eventually experience the reward in His perfect timing. Are you a student, on the other hand? Then, your primary purpose is to study, learn, perform well in school, finish your degree, find a job and eventually get married someday.

Remember the parable of the three servants in Matthew 25:14-30 wherein a master entrusted bags of silver to his three men? When he returned home, he was pleased with the first two because they used their capabilities to multiply the money. Meanwhile, he despised the third servant because he just buried the bags into the ground and returned it to him without any earnings. Just as this master, God entrusted us gifts and blessings (our talents, skills, and capabilities) and He wants us to use them and make our fortune grow. Your purpose is to be a good steward of what you have no matter how small it is so that God will entrust you with bigger blessings in the future.

To be healthy and wise

Our body is the temple of the Holy Spirit and our role is to take good care of it not just to accomplish our daily tasks but most importantly, to use our body in fulfilling our purpose. We needed a healthy body and mind to be able to follow the right path clearly and to be able to achieve the plans of God for us.

Chapter 2: Your Five Spiritual Purposes

According to Genesis 1:27, we are created through the image and likeness of God and that's why we should also consider our spiritual life because among the two purposes, your spiritual purpose is the most important because your spirit is eternal. This means that your life still continues even after you become separated from your physical body.

Here are the lists of our spiritual purposes designed by the Creator Himself.

To glorify and praise God

"Yet a time is coming and has now come when the true worshippers will worship the Father in the Spirit and in truth, for they are the kind of worshipers the Father seeks. God is Spirit, and his worshipers must worship in the Spirit and in truth." –JOHN 4:23-24

We were born and created by God for his glory and purpose. We are specially designed by Him among all of His other creations because we are created in His image and likeness and He treated us as His own children. So, whenever you feel down and insignificant, remember that your life is important and precious in His eyes because He created you for His pleasure. One of the purposes of our existence is to worship and praise him. But it doesn't mean singing or playing instruments alone. The Bible clearly stated that in everything we do, we should do it for the glory of God. So, whether you are typing your financial report, writing a homework article or cooking your favorite meal, do it for the Lord. Fulfill it as if you are actually serving God. We can turn our everyday activities as acts of worship.

To receive His gift of salvation

"For God so loved the world, he gave his only Son and whoever believes in him shall not perish but have an everlasting life." - John 3:16

Since everyone falls short of God's glory, God sent His Only Son, Jesus to redeem us from death and punishment. And you are destined to receive this marvelous gift from the Lord and to live your life according to His purpose and plans. He sent His Son, so we could be redeemed from the eternal damnation. And because of Christ, we were all set free! Thus, God wants us to walk in righteousness and be like Jesus who already overcame the world.

To live a progressive Christian life

"We are not meant to remain as children" –Ephesians 4:14

Once you became a Christian and you received God's eternal salvation, our purpose now is to live a sanctified life. We have to become a true living testimony of God to others. It doesn't mean that we should do nothing at all since we are already saved. But rather, we must consider now how to live differently with the guidance of the Lord. Thus, we have to live for the development and growth of our spiritual relationship with God. And in order to that, life offers three tools for us:

1. **THE BIBLE** – Everything we need to know about life can be found in the Bible. That's why it is considered as the light to our path because it really leads us towards the light of God.

2. **CHURCH** – The primary reason why an individual must find his own church is to sustain his spiritual growth. He needs church fellowship to encourage him when he feels down and to rejoice with him whenever he is happy. Above all, he needs the church so that he can have a family that is always ready and

willing to pray for him. Nobody will grow alone spiritually. Fellowship is very important towards your spiritual growth and the place to perform your ministry to the Lord.

3. **SUFFERING** – Trials and difficulties are tools to make us strong. It is not true that being a Christian means you won't be facing anymore problems in life. In fact, God actually allows certain storms to test and strengthen our faith. Our purpose is to overcome these trials and most of all to exalt the name of the Lord upon our victory.

To serve God

"God has given each of you some special abilities; be sure to use them to help each other, passing on to others God's many kinds of blessings." -1 Peter 4:10

You were created to use your abilities to serve God's kingdom. It is not enough that we sit and listen from the benches of our church every Sunday. Let us use our different talents and gifts as our ministry. Are you good at music? Then dedicate your music to the Lord and participate in music ministry! In this way, you can bring back all the glory to Him alone. Are you a business-minded person and good at making money?

Then, support your church finances and be a channel of blessings to your brothers and sisters who need your help. In almost every way, you can actually serve God's purpose based on your own abilities.

To share the good news of salvation

"Go and make disciples of all nations, baptizing them in the name of the Father, and of the Son and of the Holy Spirit, and teaching them to obey everything I have commanded you. And surely, I am with you always, to the very end of the age." - Matthew 28:19-20

Since we are chosen by the Lord to become His children and followers, it is our mission to spread the good news of salvation to the others. It should be our priority to let others know their purpose here on earth. It is our responsibility to introduce Jesus Christ as their own and personal Savior and the only way towards the eternal life because as He said, *"I am the way, the truth and the life. No one can come to the Father but through me."*

However, to put these unbelievers in conviction is not our place. It is the Holy Spirit's job. So, don't feel bad if the outcome of your sharing didn't turn out the way you wanted it to happen. By planting the seed into their hearts, we have done our part and fulfilled this purpose already. Through faithful and continuous prayers, let Christ work on your behalf. Sometimes it will take days, months or even few long years before this planted seed grows but as long as you keep planting it everywhere, you know the harvesting is possible and it will come in due time.

Chapter 3: When Finding Your Purpose Becomes Difficult

Now, with some of these pointers about your real purposes, you still may find it very difficult to actually stick to them all the time. However, a freeing thought is to simply remember that life is actually not about us after all. The root in finding and fulfilling life's purpose is to simply love God above all things. In that manner, we won't get tired and get sick of doing the same things every day. *"Everything comes from God alone. Everything lives by his power, and everything is for his glory." (Romans 11:36)* Let us make sure that in everything we do, we are pleasing God.

We must not base our worship with our feelings and emotions. A lot of people deceive themselves if they are thinking that worshipping and praising God is about feeling good all the time. Thus, when they are sad or disappointed, it's now hard for them to offer Him praises. Even if God seems very far away, our faith should not be shaken. For God is true to His promises even if we don't feel His presence. We must continue to praise and glorify Him even if we don't feel like it. Worship doesn't work as a self-fulfillment mechanism. We worship not because we want to feel better. We worship because God deserves it and if you learn to think and see it that way, you won't give Him praises that are only second best.

When spiritual dryness occupies your whole being, it would be very difficult to continue living your life with a purpose. It is by then we should start trusting the will of the Lord. This simply means you should walk by faith and not by sight. God said in Hebrews 13:5, *"I will never leave you nor forsake you"*. So, if you feel weak and discouraged by the storms that you are facing in your life and you are failing to fulfill your purpose, ask for God's guidance, strength and wisdom to overcome such hindrances. Our God is a faithful God who keeps His promises. Long before you were born, He knows your strength and capabilities. He is absolutely certain that you are stronger than you ever dreamed of. In every season of our lives, He is still God and He is your Creator and for that, we still have the reason to sing and worship him in Spirit and in truth.

Just remember these three important steps to continue your journey towards fulfilling your life's purpose:

1. **Acknowledge your Creator** – Know that God is always longing for your praises and He has better and concrete plans waiting for you whether it is physically or spiritually. Just as he said in Jeremiah 1:5, *"Before I formed you in the womb, I knew you, before you were born I set you apart."*

2. **Acknowledge your limited time** – remember that your life here on Earth is too short to just waste it wandering around and doing nothing or useless things. Time is like a rainbow, you have to make the most of it before it fades. For it is written, *"How do you know what your life will be like tomorrow? Your life is like the morning fog--it's here a little while, then it's gone."* –James 4:14

3. **Acknowledge your blessings** – Let's focus on our life's blessings and choose not to focus on our failures and disappointments. With that, giving praises to the Lord will be so much easier! Meanwhile, it is better if we can also see the trials and hardships as blessing for our faith and strength. *"Blessed is the one who perseveres under trials because, having stood the test, that person will receive the crown of life that the Lord has promised to those who love him."* –James 1:12

Chapter 4: Showing Off Your Purpose

Now that we've learned the true purposes of life, we must learn how to live with it. It is our role to make it shine as far as we can to be able to influence the lives of others. We don't want to just discover our purpose and then keep it hidden, right? After all, we are meant to exalt our Creator's name!

Isn't it great that even before you speak of God's words and purpose to the others, people can actually see and understand it through your actions first? Let's put it this way--- how can you tell your friends that God's plans and purpose for us is to achieve our personal dreams when you can't even reach your own goals in life yourself? Be a living testimony of God and the rest will follow according to his richness and glory.

Don't be afraid to show off your true life's existence. Who knows one of these coming days; you are bound to inspire someone else's life with your own life story and history. So, keep your light shining and be ready to share your life's purpose!

"Finally, brethren, whatever is true, whatever is honorable, whatever is right, whatever is pure, whatever is lovely, whatever is of good repute, if there is any excellence and if anything worthy of praise, let your mind dwell on these things" - *Philippians 4:8*

Conclusion

Thank you for buying this book! I really hope it helped summarize our Christian Purpose in life. I know it sometimes feels very difficult to comprehend and define. It's like seeking out a needle from the whole stack of hay. And because of our sins, many things in life may lead us into deception if we don't stay vigilant and alert. That's why it is important that we are always guided and equipped by God's words.

Physical and spiritual purposes are two different things, yet both of these come from the Lord. These two things were both created to simply praise and honor God alone. True Christian living is about living every aspect of your life in harmony and perfect balance. So, if ever you've been blessed by God to achieve your financial purpose, you must be experiencing the same spiritual fulfillment at the same time. That's how life is supposed to be! You must keep it in balance to be able to bring true glory and honor to its one and only Author!

"Finally, dear brothers and sisters, we urge you in the name of the Lord Jesus to live in a way that pleases God, as we have taught you. You live this way already, and we encourage you to do so even more." -1 Thessalonians 4:4

Thanks again, and good luck! Oh also, if you enjoyed this book, please take the time to share your thoughts and post a review on Amazon. It'd be greatly appreciated!

Introducing my book 'Disciplining a Defiant Child'

If you have a child who's defiant or disobedient, and you want help figuring out how to discipline them and get them back on the right life path, you may be interested in this book. As parents, it's our ministry to lead our Children to God and to raise them to become better people and contribute to society in a positive way, living in a manner that pleases the Lord. As I explain in this book, there are lots of tips and tricks to keep in mind during those situations when our children exhibit bad attitudes or are disobedient, and we almost lose our cool. Join me for this short read, and your children will be back on the right path in no time!

Here's the link for my book 'Disciplining a Defiant Child':
http://www.amazon.com/dp/B00KJQSNB8/

Printed in Great Britain
by Amazon